how to match
food and wine

how to match
food and wine

a comprehensive guide
to choosing wine to go
with food

MITCHELL BEAZLEY

fiona beckett

how to match food and wine
by fiona beckett

First published in Great Britain in 2002
by Mitchell Beazley, an imprint of Octopus
Publishing Group Limited, 2–4 Heron Quays,
London E14 4JP.

A CIP catalogue record for this book is
available from the British Library.

ISBN: 1 84000 576 9

Commissioning editor   Rebecca Spry
Executive art editor   Yasia Williams
Photographer   Alan Williams
Managing editor   Emma Rice
Design   Nicky Collings
Editor   Susan Keevil
Production   Alix McCulloch
Index   Ann Barrett

Mitchell Beazley would like to thank Denbies
Wine Estate, Surrey and Majestic Wine
Warehouse, Chalk Farm and Docklands for the
use of their premises for the photography.

Typeset in RotisSansSerif

Printed and bound by
Toppan Printing Company in China

contents

introduction

Matching food with wine is not quite like matching a pair of shoes or socks. There's no right or wrong about it, it's just that some combinations are more enjoyable than others. It's like cooking. Some partnerships – tomatoes and basil, grilled fish and lemon, strawberries and cream – just gel. Wine is like an extra ingredient that finishes a dish off. Over the following pages you'll find suggestions that should act as starting points. What to order in the many ethnic restaurants we now have. What to drink with your favourite dishes from roast chicken to chocolate cake. Safe choices and more experimental ones. And finally, food to flatter that extra special bottle. The great thing is you never stop learning. Just as you improvise with recipes, one day you'll try out an unfamiliar wine with a dish and "Eureka!", it'll be amazing. Just remember: choosing wine shouldn't be a worry. And drinking it should be fun.

There are reasons why some wines work better than others with the food you're eating and while you probably don't want to think it through from first principles every time, it can help to know what they are:

how the books works

Some red grapes

Barbera, Bonarda, Cabernet Franc, Carmenère, Cinsaut, Dolcetto, Gamay, Grenache, Kékfrankos, Madiran, Malbec, Mourvèdre, Nebbiolo, Negroamaro, Pinotage, Primitivo, Ruby Cabernet, Sangiovese, Shiraz/Syrah, Tannat, Tarrango, Tempranillo, Zinfandel

Some white grapes

Arneis, Chasselas, Chenin Blanc, Colombard, Gewurztraminer, Grenache Blanc, Marsanne, Muscat, Pinot Blanc/Pinot Bianco, Pinot Gris/Pinot Grigio, Riesling, Roussanne, Semillon, Torrontés, Verdelho, Viognier

What type of food it is

Less important than you might think. Obviously, fish calls for a different type of wine to, say, a fruit tart. And white meat is generally better with white wine than red meat. But you can't make a judgment on the type of wine to drink purely by knowing what type of protein it is. It also depends...

How it's cooked

Or not cooked. The temperature that food is served at is also important. Cold food needs lighter wine than hot food. So whether it's meat or fish, chilled dry whites and rosés, and light, fruity (preferably chilled) reds work best.

Once the heat is on, a whole range of different factors come into play. Different cooking methods make some foods turn out less robust than others, even when the main ingredient is the same. For instance, if a dish is boiled, steamed, or microwaved, it will need a less sturdy wine than if it's grilled or roasted or barbecued. High cooking temperatures call for more alcoholic wines.

It also depends how long it's cooked. Food cooked for a short time (stir-fried, seared, deep-fried) suits lighter wines than food which is braised or pot roasted. Though it depends...

How it's seasoned

Common sense really but the more robust the flavouring the more full-bodied the wine you need. So steamed fish would need a more characterful white if it was seasoned Chinese style with spring onions, soy, garlic, and sesame oil, than if it were served plain. You also need to take account of...

What it's served with

Your food may be plainly cooked but if it's served with flavoursome veg like red cabbage or ratatouille, these will affect your wine choice. The classic is Christmas dinner, where the accompaniments require a more powerful red than you'd need for the turkey alone (see page 44).

Difficult? Not really

To sum it up, light wines suit light food, and robust gutsy food calls for robust wine. A guideline that's far handier than the old "white wine with fish, red wine with meat" rule.

Whatever the food involved certain flavours crop up again and again. You may not think of a dish first and foremost as, say, a salty or a sour one, but if that character predominates it can significantly affect your wine choice.

six key food flavours

Salty

Inherently salty food like anchovies, oysters, and other shellfish goes best with crisp, dry white wines such as Muscadet and Chablis, and with equally tangy manzanilla sherry. Neutral whites also go well with salt beef and salt cod. Adding salt to food is a useful trick to use to make oaky reds seem less tannic.

Sour/sharp

Foods that are dominated by the taste of lemon, lime, or vinegar can be quite difficult to match with wine. A wine with a good level of acidity of its own such as a Sauvignon Blanc, Riesling, or a light Italian red such as Valpolicella tends to work best. Squeezing lemon juice onto a dish can also make full-bodied whites or reds taste less oaky.

Savoury

The kind of flavour you find in mushrooms, soy, smoked meats like bacon, aged Parmesan, concentrated meat reductions – referred to by the Japanese as "umami"– is the best kind of match for medium- to full-bodied reds. It's much less good with whites.

Spicy

Food spiced by chillies or peppercorns reduces the sweetness of any wine that accompanies it, so it can make dry reds like Bordeaux taste quite astringent. It also accentuates obvious oak flavours. The best wines to pair with spicy food are unoaked or lightly oaked ones, with plenty of ripe, juicy fruit.

Smoky

Smoked foods need a wine with a strong enough personality to cope with their powerful flavours. Dry fino or manzanilla sherry is generally a safe choice but, oddly, a touch of sweetness can work well too. German Kabinett Rieslings are good, for example, with smoked fish and meats, especially pork. With smoky barbecue sauces it's best to choose a powerful red wine such as a Shiraz or Zinfandel.

Sweet

Sweetness in a dish makes any wine seem drier. Sweet wines should always be sweeter than the dessert they accompany or they'll taste thin and sour. With savoury dishes that contain fruity or sweet elements such as honey, or a cranberry or lingonberry sauce, that isn't always possible but at least make sure your wine is one that has some good lush fruit of its own.

Red wine names

Amarone, Bandol, Banyuls, Barbaresco, Barolo, Bourgueil, Cahors, Chambolle-Musigny, Chorey-lès-Beaune, Copertino, Costières de Nîmes, Côte-Rôtie, Crozes-Hermitage, Faugères, Gigondas, Madiran, Marsannay, Maury, Mavrodaphne, Minervois, Montepulciano d'Abruzzo, Pic St Loup, Pomerol, Ribera del Duero, Rully, St-Chinian, St-Emilion, Salice Salentino, Saumur-Champigny, Sassicaia, Teroldego Rotaliano, Tignanello, Valpolicella, Vosne-Romanée

White wine names

Albariño, Asti, Barsac, Bianco di Custoza, Gavi, Lugana, Monbazillac, Moscatel de Valencia, Moscato di Pantelleria, Orvieto, Picpoul-de-Pinet, Premières Côtes de Bordeaux, Rueda, Saussignac, Soave, Tokáji, Verdicchio, Vermentino, Vin Santo, Vinho Verde

world food

We live in an age where we can eat every kind of cuisine and partner it with almost every possible kind of wine. But in most countries people still stick to what they know. A Frenchman wouldn't dream of drinking a wine from outside his region never mind the rest of world. Nor would an Italian. I'm a firm believer in adopting a "when in Rome" attitude – drinking whatever the locals drink when I'm in a wine-producing country or region, being prepared to experiment when I eat the same food somewhere else.

In countries such as France and Italy it's easy to find a bottle to go with what you're eating. It's food from a country like Thailand with no tradition of wine and where different dishes are served at the same time where problems can arise. Keep an open mind!

Eating around the world

Italy

Wine in Italy is as regional as its food – from the simple, quaffable Pinot Grigios that seem made to go with the seafood of Venice, to the young vibrant Dolcettos you drink with the truffle-laden pasta dishes of Piedmont.

With antipasti, fishy pastas, and seafood neutral Italian whites are the ideal partners. Less well-known names that offer good value are Vernaccia di San Gimignano, Verdicchio dei Castelli di Jesi, Bianco di Custoza, and Orvieto.

With simple roasts and grills bitter cherry-flavoured reds such as Barbera, Dolcetto, and Valpolicella work well, as does (much more reliable than it used to be) Chianti. Try these wines with pasta dishes too (see Pasta, page 30).

With red meats and cheese dark, figgy southern Italian reds such as Negroamaro go well. So do Italian grapes grown elsewhere such as Sangiovese, Barbera, and Bonarda from Australia, Argentina, and California.

Other wines to try: when dining Italian style, or eating in an Italian restaurant abroad, look out for wines from underrated regions such as Umbria, the Marches, southern Italy, and Sicily.

France

France is another country where you'll always get the best value if you drink the local wine. Don't be afraid to buy direct – as the French do – from local growers and cooperatives.

With oysters or other fresh seafood drink a Muscadet, Petit Chablis, inexpensive white Bordeaux, or other Sauvignon Blanc.

With pâté or other charcuterie a light red such as Beaujolais, or a simple red *vin de pays*.

With creamy sauces try a white Burgundy, Languedoc Chardonnay, or Viognier, or an Alsace Riesling or Pinot Gris.

With coq au vin, daubes, and other dishes cooked with wine: a similar wine to that used in the dish. Southern French reds such as Corbières, Faugères, Fitou, Minervois, and St-Chinian suit bistro cooking well.

With French patisserie: good-value sweet wines such as Coteaux du Layon, Monbazillac, Saussignac, and southern French Muscats.

Drinking Italian

Kick off the meal with a glass of **Prosecco** – Italy's best inexpensive sparkling wine.

Order a **Vin Santo** and **cantucci** (dipping biscuits) instead of a dessert.

Finish with a **grappa** to help digest your meal.

In a French restaurant or bar

Try one of France's many aperitifs – Chambéry, Lillet from Bordeaux, Pernod, Pastis, or Suze.

Don't be embarrassed to drink rosé, especially in the south where it's more popular than white.

Experiment with combinations of regional French wines and cheeses such as Chaource and Champagne, Munster and Gewurztraminer, and Crottin de Chavignol and Sancerre.

Spain

Rosé (*rosado*) and red wines are more popular in Spain than white or even Spain's best-known wine, sherry. Young (*joven*) or *crianza* wines (aged for a year in oak) are more **flexible** with food and cheaper than aged *reserva* or *gran reservas*.

With spicy tapas and seafood chilled fino or manzanilla.

With grilled fish and rice dishes such as paella try Spain's most interesting white wine, Albariño, a Rueda, or an unoaked white Rioja.

With lamb (Spain's most popular meat), pork, suckling pig try Ribera del Duero, Rioja, or red from neighbouring Navarra.

Other wines to try: Argentinian Tempranillo (the same grape you find in Rioja). Red wines from the Rhône and Languedoc also work well with Spanish meat dishes.

Portugal

As its extensive coastline suggests, Portugal's cuisine does feature a lot of seafood, but it contains more meat-based dishes than you might imagine.

With red meat and game choose a red from the up-and-coming Alentejo and Douro – the latter is the same region that produces port.

With seafood drink a spritzy white Vinho Verde or a new wave Portuguese white.

Scandinavia

The sweet-sour flavour of pickled fish like herring is the main stumbling block for the Scandinavian wine drinker. Lager, aquavit, or schnapps is the local solution but Alsace Riesling, or dry German Kabinett or Spätlese Riesling, should get you by, too. California or New Zealand Pinot Noir works well with game such as reindeer and venison.

Germany

Unsurprisingly, Germany's fine dry Rieslings suit German food – from cured and smoked meats, to delicate creamy-sauced trout, and rustic dishes such as sauerkraut. Sweeter Rieslings go perfectly with apple- and lemon-based desserts, but the sweetest of all – Trockenbeerenauslese and Eiswein – are best sipped on their own. Modern German reds such as Spätburgunder are excellent with German-style roast meats – as would be many other classic European reds.

Greece, Turkey, and Lebanon

There are differences between the cuisines of each of these countries, the structure of the meals – hot and cold mezze, followed by grilled meat or fish – and the palate of flavours is similar. It's a style of cooking that suits the excellent fresh, crisp white wines that are now coming out of Greece as well as other dry whites from around the Mediterranean.

Meat and richly flavoured aubergine dishes take well to the new soft, fruity Greek reds and to mature, oak-aged Lebanese reds such as Chateau Musar.

In western Greece and islands such as Corfu and Cephalonia, where the food is more influenced by Italy, the food also tastes good with Italian wines.

What else can you drink with this style of food? Syrah and Tempranillo based reds. Australian whites such as Verdelho.

Tunisia and Morocco

A slightly spicier register of flavours which suits the vibrant new Moroccan and Tunisian reds now emerging – based on similar grapes to those that grow in southern France. Spanish and Portuguese reds work well, too, with couscous and tagines.

Thailand and Southeast Asia

The hot/sour elements in Thai food lead in the direction of white rather than red wine. Aromatic whites such as

Australian or New Zealand Riesling, or Alsace Pinot Gris and Gewurztraminer are good companions – just as they are to milder Vietnamese food. Semillon and Sauvignon Blanc (especially Australian and New Zealand Sauvignon) work well too. If you prefer red, make it vibrant and fruity – inexpensive Shiraz blends, Merlot, Ruby Cabernet.

China

Fruity rosés and light reds such as Beaujolais and inexpensive New World reds, are more flexible than aromatic whites such as Gewurztraminer and Riesling – the wines most commonly recommended with Chinese food. Pinot Noir is a great match for crispy duck. Sauvignon Blanc works with seafood and deep-fried dishes such as spring rolls, so it's a useful bottle to have on the table at the start of a meal. Sparkling wine – white or rosé – is also good with dim sum: Champagne's a great option, if you're feeling extravagant!

Japan

Japan's is not the easiest cuisine to match with wine. The Japanese have a taste for Chablis and top Bordeaux but tend to pair these with classic French food. Otherwise they usually drink beer. Very dry whites such as Chablis and Muscadet work well with raw fish dishes such as sushi and sashimi, as does *blanc de blancs* Champagne. Sparkling wine is good with tempura too. Meatier dishes prepared on a Teppanyaki grill or with a teriyaki sauce, suit medium-bodied fruity reds such as Chilean Merlot.

Antipodean wines to drink with Asian food

Having grown up hand in hand with it, Australian and Kiwi wines are some of the best bottles to drink with Asian food:

Australian sparkling Chardonnay

Australian and New Zealand Riesling

Australian and New Zealand Sauvignon Blanc

Australian rosé

New Zealand Pinot Noir

Inexpensive Shiraz (save pricier bottles for less challenging flavours).

India

Heat is the litmus test with Indian food. If the dish is very, very hot you're better off drinking lager – or lassi. But with the majority of dishes, New World whites such as Australian Semillon/Chardonnay, or Australian or South African Colombard, and soft fruity reds such as inexpensive Shiraz or Shiraz/Cabernet, work perfectly well. Portuguese reds are surprisingly good. Avoid full-bodied, high-alcohol reds which increase the sensation of heat on the palate. With milder dishes you can also drink crisp, dry whites and rosés, and even sparkling wine makes a good match, especially with street-style food.

North America

Although vines are grown all over the States, nowhere has as sophisticated a food and wine culture as does California. There you can find every kind of cuisine (the influences are mainly Mediterranean and Asian) and wines to go with it. With seafood, salads, and vegetable dishes drink Sauvignon Blanc (softer and less herbaceous than elsewhere in the wine world), Chardonnay, and Viognier.

Star home grown reds for meat dishes are Pinot Noir (which will also go with fish), Zinfandel (Calfiornia's own red grape), and top-class Cabernet Sauvignon and Merlot. Look out for these last two from Washington State too.

Central and South America

Mexico has great food but not much wine to speak of. Chile and Argentina have great wine but their food isn't too hot (apart from the steaks).
solution: drink South American wines with Mexican food – Sauvignon Blanc with seafood; blackcurranty Cabernet Sauvignon, plummy Merlot, and Malbec with beef and lamb dishes.

The Caribbean

Beer and cocktail-drinking territory but again, South American whites and reds will ride to the rescue with the spicy cuisine.

Cal-Ital

They may not have hit the shelves in any numbers yet but watch out for a new raft of Italian-inspired wines from California, such as Sangiovese, to match the US passion for Italian cuisine.
In the meantime you'll find that Italian wines – reds in particular – taste great with Cal-Ital food.

greatest hits

Think of the ingredients you enjoy most – from pasta to salad to (everyone's favourite) chocolate. Now think of the multitude of different ways you prepare them. Here's an easy-to-use guide to what to drink with all your favourite foods.

Thinking of starters as mini versions of main courses – which is often exactly what they are – makes it easier to decide what to drink with them. A small portion of salmon calls for the same type of wine as a large one. Having said that, lighter, fresher wines will generally work better at this stage of a meal than weighing your palate down with richer, more full-bodied ones.

soups & starters

Sherry

Traditionally paired with soup, bone-dry, well-chilled, fino or manzanilla sherry is actually better with seafood. Try it with smoked salmon, squid, or fried or grilled fish. And, of course, tapas such as olives, nuts, air-dried ham, and spicy chorizo sausage.

To be honest, you don't need to drink wine with soup unless it's got ravioli or something else extravagant floating around in it. But here's what works if you do want to:

Thin soups and broths
safe bets: classic Rhône or modern Languedoc white grape blends (spicy, flavoursome mixtures of Roussanne, Marsanne, and Viognier grapes.)
adventurous alternatives: if it's an Asian-inspired soup or broth, try New Zealand Sauvignon Blanc, or an Australian Verdelho.

Thick chunky soups like minestrone
safe bets: if there are a lot of green vegetables in it try a dry Italian white like Soave. If it includes tomato and garlic, or beans, or lentils, go for a robust southern French, Italian, Spanish, or Portuguese red.

Seafood soups, and stews like bouillabaisse

safe bets: generally best with crisp, dry whites – the kind
you find in Provence and elsewhere in southern France
– or with an inexpensive Sauvignon Blanc.
adventurous alternatives: Picpoul de Pinet – a dry
Muscadet-like wine from the Languedoc in southern
France – or a Spanish Albariño.

Chowders and other creamy soups

safe bets: unoaked or lightly oaked Chardonnay or South
African Chenin Blanc.
adventurous alternatives: Viognier, or New Zealand or
Oregon Pinot Gris.

Gazpacho and other cold soups

safe bets: inexpensive Spanish whites such as unoaked
white Rioja. Or, if you're willing to spend a bit more,
try an Albariño.

Like vegetables, salads generally only determine your wine choice when they're the main course rather than a side dish or part of a salad selection. As light, summery food they call for summery wines such as crisp, dry whites and rosés, though if you dress them with a punchy dressing you'll need a more gutsy wine to cope.

salads & dressings

Zip and zest

Just as a salad needs a dressing it also needs a wine with a bit of zip and zest. Unoaked fruity whites and soft fruity reds work better than rich, oaky or delicate, mature wines.

Light vegetable and seafood salads

safe bets: citrussy Sauvignon works well, particularly if the salad contains asparagus. Rosé is ideal with salade niçoise.
adventurous alternatives: dry English whites.

Caesar salad, salads with chicken, or cheese

safe bets: unoaked Chardonnay, or Chardonnay/Semillon blends. South African Chenin Blanc.

Tomato, mozzarella and basil, and other antipasti salads

safe bets: dry Italian whites such as Pinot Grigio, Soave, Orvieto, and Verdicchio.
adventurous options: Spanish Rueda, unoaked white Rioja.

Asian flavours – spicy-flavoured dressings

safe bets: off-dry Australian Riesling, Semillon, or Verdelho.
adventurous alternative: Argentinian Torrontés.

Warm salads with duck, or pigeon breast, or chicken livers

safe bet: young New World Pinot Noir works particularly well. California and New Zealand provide the best value.
adventurous alternatives: German or Austrian reds.

Gutsy salads with grilled vegetables or a spicy or garlicky dressing

safe bet: a soft, medium-bodied red such as Chilean Merlot.
adventurous alternative: a fruity California Zinfandel.

Three traps for salad eaters...

Sharp vinaigrette dressings can murder the taste of good wine. If you're drinking something serious, make your dressing with a little wine or chicken stock instead of vinegar. A dash of walnut or hazelnut oil can also make a dressing more wine-friendly.

Raw onion and garlic can be killers. Keep your wine choice cheap and cheerful – something like a Vin de Pays des Côtes de Gascogne, inexpensive Sauvignon, or Chilean or Australian rosé.

Blue cheese dressings are hard for any wine to cope with. Your best bet is to blast through them with intensely rich, jammy Australian or Chilean reds, which have a touch of sweetness.

Picnics

Temperature is the most important thing to remember about wine for picnics. Whether it's white, red, rosé – or even a bottle of bubbly – keep it cool. If you chill your bottle before setting out, then put it in an insulated bag or jacket, it should be at just the right temperature by the time you arrive. Remember, everything tastes more muted when you're out in the open so go for wines with obvious fruity flavours. New World or southern French rosés are perfect.

I'm not suggesting serving wine with breakfast, but wine with eggs can be surprisingly good. I say surprising because the conventional wisdom used to be that wine didn't go with eggs at all – it was the runny yolks that were supposed to destroy it. But I've enjoyed red Bordeaux with bacon and eggs, and Meursault with eggs benedict without either wine suffering. And Champagne goes brilliantly with most egg dishes.

eggs, eggs, & eggs

Brunch

Unless you're sticking strictly to breakfast dishes your brunch will probably contain more robust flavours than eggs alone. Nonetheless, Champagne (or a cheap sparkling wine such as cava) is a good way to kick off – diluted half and half with fresh orange juice to make a Buck's Fizz, if everyone's feeling fragile. After that I'd lay on some bottles of unoaked Chardonnay and a light, fruity red such as Merlot.

Scrambled eggs

safe bets: Sparkling Chardonnay or *blanc de blancs* Champagne – particularly if the eggs include smoked salmon.

adventurous alternative: a Sardinian Vermentino.

Eggs benedict

safe bets: the hollandaise sauce is the problem, but a good-quality, oaked Chardonnay or Champagne (preferably vintage!) should do the trick. As would an Alsace Pinot Blanc.

adventurous alternatives: a southern French or California Roussanne.

Omelettes and quiches

safe bets: it depends to some extent on the other ingredients involved, but an unoaked or lightly oaked Chardonnay, Alsace Pinot Blanc, or smooth, dry Italian

white like Soave, would work with most quiches.
adventurous alternatives: dry Alsace or Clare Valley
(Australian) Rieslings.

Eggs with ham or bacon, or with spicy tomato sauce (huevos rancheros)

safe bets: Chablis – or a basic Bourgogne Blanc.
adventurous alternatives: a light, fruity red such as an
inexpensive young Bordeaux, Rioja, or Merlot, has the
edge on white wine here. Choose a gutsier southern
French red for *oeufs en meurette* (cooked in red wine).

Pasta is such a regular part of all of our diets that we probably grab whatever wine we have to hand to match it. But if you want to be a bit more adventurous, bear in mind that creamy, light, vegetable (eg asparagus), and fishy sauces go best with white wines, and tomato- or meat-based ones go better with red. And always match the wine to the sauce rather than the pasta shape!

pasta, polenta, & noodles

Spaghetti carbonara and other creamy sauces
safe bets: Soave, Bianco di Custoza, Pinot Bianco, Italian Chardonnay.
adventurous alternative: Vin de Pays d'Oc Viognier.

Spaghetti alla vongole and other fishy sauces (see also Posh pasta)
safe bets: Pinot Grigio, Frascati, or an inexpensive Italian Chardonnay.
adventurous alternatives: unoaked Greek whites match the feisty fishy flavours with a zip of their own; or try Chilean or California Sauvignon Blanc, or Chablis.

Spaghetti al limone
safe bets: Verdicchio dei Castelli di Jesi, Orvieto.
adventurous alternatives: Grenache Blanc from the Languedoc, Valpolicella.

Pasta alla genovese (with green pesto)

safe bets: Gavi, Soave, Bianco di Custoza, light Chardonnay.
adventurous alternatives: Albariño (from Spain), any
unoaked Chardonnay. (With pasta dressed in red pesto
you'll probably enjoy a soft, medium-bodied red like
Merlot more.)

Bolognese and other meaty pasta sauces

safe bets: decent Chianti, good Valpolicella.
adventurous alternatives: California Zinfandel,
Côtes du Roussillon and other southern French reds,
Tempranillo from Spain.

Napoletana and other tomato-based sauces

safe bets: Montepulciano d'Abruzzo, Barbera.
adventurous alternative: Hungarian Merlot.

Puttanesca and other gutsy sauces with anchovies, olives, or capers

safe bet: a Sicilian or southern Italian red such
as Negroamaro.
adventurous alternatives: Argentinian Bonarda or Syrah.

Lasagne, cannelloni, and other baked pastas

safe bets: it depends what they're layered or stuffed with.
If they're meaty, go for the same type of wine as Bolognese
(above). With spinach and ricotta try a dry Italian white
such as Soave. Or if the dish is based on mushrooms, a
light Italian red such as Dolcetto.

Posh pasta

Pasta doesn't have to
be basic everyday food –
it can be quite ritzy.
If seafood, like lobster,
crab, or scallops, is involved
try a good Chardonnay. If
it's garnished with truffles
you could drink a Barolo,
red Burgundy or other
Pinot Noir. And if it's
adorned with caviar there's
always Champagne.

Peasant pasta

If you were in Italy you'd undoubtedly drink the local vino with your pasta, so don't feel embarrassed to pull out a cheap and cheerful wine. Regions like Puglia in southern Italy, and Sicily, are providing some of the best-drinking bargains at the moment.

adventurous alternatives: (with spinach) trendy Spanish white, Albariño; (with mushrooms) California or New Zealand Pinot Noir.

Ravioli and other stuffed pastas

Again, it depends what they're stuffed with (*see* above, and Posh pasta on previous page.)

Pasta salads

safe bets: Soave, light Italian Chardonnay.
adventurous alternatives: South African Chenin Blanc, Australian dry whites.

Noodles

Most noodle dishes are based on Asian flavours so suit assertive New World wines best. White grape varieties like Sauvignon Blanc, Semillon, Verdelho, and Riesling work well, particularly from Australia where this type of food has worked its way into the culture. And if the dish forms part of a Chinese meal you might like to try a fruity rosé (*see* page 19).

Polenta

Unless it is accompanied by strongly flavoured meat (*see* page 38) try one of the following:
safe bets: light Italian reds like young Nebbiolo or Dolcetto.
adventurous alternatives: Chilean Carmenère or Merlot.

As with pasta, the way rice and grains are cooked matters more than their basic flavour. Many dishes are representative of an ethnic cuisine so be guided by the cooking style (*see* World Food).

rice & grains

Risotto
safe bets: most dry Italian whites (except oaky Chardonnay). If made with red wine, try light, red Dolcetto, or Valpolicella. *adventurous alternatives:* Sauvignon if with spring vegetables; unoaked Chardonnay with shellfish; Pinot Noir with mushroom.

Paella
safe bets: Spanish rosé, unoaked white Rioja, or Tempranillo. *adventurous alternatives:* Rhône or Languedoc whites, or rosés.

Biryani and pilaus
safe bets: unless accompanied by other hotter dishes (*see* page 20) any inexpensive dry white or rosé, eg *vin de pays*. *adventurous alternatives:* Indian sparkling, cava, Viognier.

Sushi
safe bets: green tea and miso soup. *adventurous alternatives:* Champagne or fizz, Muscadet and (I'm assured by a Japanese friend) red Burgundy.

Most fish has a delicate flavour that isn't going to overpower any wine. And if it's ultra-fresh and simply cooked you don't want to swamp it in return. Most dry whites will work so your choice is more likely to be determined by the occasion and how much you want to spend. Once you start introducing other ingredients – like tomato and garlic, or lime and coriander, or use more robust cooking techniques such as chargrilling or barbecuing, you'll need wines that will stand up to these stronger flavours as you'll see from the suggestions below.

fish, from river to sea

Five fish-friendly wines

Sauvignon Blanc – grilled, oily fish, Asian flavours.

Muscadet – oysters and other raw seafood.

Chablis – simply cooked fish: the classic choice.

White Burgundy – richly sauced fish and seafood.

Pinot Noir – seared salmon or tuna.

Fine fish like halibut, turbot, and sea bass

safe bets: Chablis, white Bordeaux, Sancerre, Pouilly-Fumé, or unoaked or subtly oaked Chardonnays.
adventurous alternative: Champagne.

Salmon

safe bet: unoaked or lightly oaked Chardonnay.
adventurous alternatives: (for seared or chargrilled salmon) Pinot Noir, Cabernet Franc, and other light reds.

Mackerel, sardines, and other oily fish

safe bet: Sauvignon Blanc.
adventurous alternatives: a sharp-flavoured, lemony Greek or Portuguese white.

Tuna, shark, and other "meaty" fish

safe bets: Australian, Chilean, or New Zealand Sauvignon or a Sauvignon blend. Unoaked New World Chardonnay.
adventurous alternatives: Pinot Noir, Cabernet Franc, and other light reds.

Trout

safe bet: light Chardonnay.
adventurous alternative: dry German Kabinett Riesling.

Raw fish, eg sushi, sashimi, raw shellfish

safe bets: very dry whites such as Muscadet or Petit Chablis.

Soused and pickled fish

Beer is, quite honestly, better than wine. Drink lager or aquavit as the Scandinavians do.

Aphrodisiac drinking

The obvious choice for a romantic dinner is Champagne, which you can happily drink through most fish-based meals, especially those which involve that ultimate aphrodisiac ingredient oysters. Sexy reds include St-Amour from the Beaujolais region (for obvious reasons), fine red Burgundy like Chambolle-Musigny, and lush ripe Merlots.

Quick-reference flavours and sauces that go with fish

Creamy sauces –
unoaked Chardonnay.

Buttery sauces –
oaked Chardonnay.

Herbs, especially dill –
Sauvignon Blanc.

Tomato- and garlic-based sauces –
Italian or southern French whites or reds.

Asian flavours –
Sauvignon Blanc, Semillon, or Riesling.

Smoked fish

safe bets: a few dry whites go well if the smoke isn't too strong – Riesling can be really good with smoked trout and salmon, as can authentic fino or manzanilla sherry, which also work with powerfully flavoured smoked mackerel.
luxury options: Champagne is a classic with smoked salmon but good dry German or Austrian Riesling is more interesting.
avoid: wine with kippers. Disgusting!

Steamed fish

safe bets: if simply cooked, try any dry white. If steamed Chinese-style with garlic and sizzling oil, go for intensely flavoured Australian or New Zealand Sauvignon.

Fried fish

safe bets: Sauvignon, Muscadet, and Pinot Grigio cut through fattiness well, but if fried in butter Chardonnay is better.
adventurous alternative: bubbles are brilliant, try cava.

Fish cakes and pies

budget buys: inexpensive Chardonnay from Eastern Europe, Italy, or the South of France, or Chile.
luxury options: with extravagant ingredients like prawns or scallops drink good Burgundy or top New World Chardonnay.

Fish stews

safe bets: with Mediterranean flavours drink dry southern French or Italian whites, or French or Spanish rosés.
adventurous alternative: Spanish Albariño.

Barbecued or spicy fish

safe bets: sharp-flavoured lemony whites (especially with oily fish like mackerel and sardines), dry rosés, light reds such as Pinot Noir.

adventurous alternatives: with "meaty" fish such as tuna, swordfish, or with really spicy marinades or seasonings, you could even drink a more robust red like a Shiraz or Merlot.

Lobster

safe bets: Premier Cru Chablis, good white Burgundy, top New World Chardonnay, or vintage Champagne.
adventurous alternative: Viognier.

Mussels

safe bets: simple dry whites like Muscadet or Pinot Grigio for *moules marinières*. For richer sauces try Chardonnay.
adventurous alternative: with spicy mussel dishes try New Zealand or Australian Sauvignon Blanc.

Oysters

safe bets: Chablis or other unoaked Chardonnay, Muscadet, or Champagne.
adventurous alternatives: New Zealand or other top Sauvignons.

Scallops

safe bet: good Chardonnay.
adventurous alternative: if served with savoury ingredients like bacon, try a light red such as Pinot Noir.

Good matches for shellfish

Most simply prepared shellfish such as crab, prawns, langoustines, and scallops, work well with Chablis and other unoaked Chardonnays, although I'd choose an even drier white like Muscadet for a classic French *plateau de fruits de mer*. For Asian-style recipes try a New World Sauvignon Blanc or Riesling.

Be in the know...

Oaky Chardonnays taste too rich with simply prepared fish and shellfish but if you add a squeeze of lemon to the dish the wine will taste fresher.

If it's meat it must be red wine. Right? Well more or less. There is nothing better than a good red wine with most meat dishes. But, like other ingredients, the ideal match also depends how you cook it, and there are dishes where white wine is just as enjoyable an option.

red & white meats

Barbecues

Powerfully sweet, smoky barbecue sauce can kill delicate wines stone dead. It's best, instead, to stick to red with plenty of juicy fruit – but not too much oak or you'll get an overload of charred, spicy flavours.

Five barbecue reds
Australian Shiraz
California Zinfandel
Chilean Cabernet
Argentinian Malbec
South African Pinotage

Cold or hot?

Cold meat suits lighter (and cooler) wines than hot meat dishes – so when you automatically reach for a chilled red or rosé in summer you'll find yourself with the right partner.

Rare or well done?

Rare meat softens tannic wines. So if you have a young oaky Cabernet Sauvignon, for example, which hasn't yet had time to mellow, serve your steak underdone – or match the young tannins by serving it well charred. Cook your meat slightly longer if you're serving an older, more fragile wine.

Plain or richly sauced?

Or, put another way, are you serving your meat with an old-fashioned gravy or a rich, sticky, concentrated *jus*? If it's the latter you'll need a more concentrated full-bodied red. In general, the meatier a dish tastes (the less disguised it is by sauce) the more classic a wine you should choose. The spicier the dish the more powerful sweet fruit you need.

Beef and steak

safe bets: most reds go with simply cooked beef. Red
Bordeaux is classic but frankly almost any good medium-
or full-bodied red – particularly Cabernet Sauvignon,
Merlot, and Syrah – will do.

adventurous alternatives: Madiran or Uruguayan Tannat,
Argentinian Malbec, red wines from the Douro in Portugal.

Raw beef dishes like carpaccio or steak tartare
safe bet: Italian reds such as Chianti Classico.
adventurous alternatives: Provençal rosé, vintage
rosé Champagne.

Homely dishes: meatloaf, casseroles, and stews
budget buys: inexpensive Cabernet Sauvignon from
Bulgaria; southern French reds such as Fitou, Corbières,
and Côtes de Roussillon; cheap Sicilian, Spanish, and
Portuguese reds.

Veal

In general suits similar types of wine to pork. Italian-style
dishes such as *scallopine* and *osso buco* work well with dry
Italian whites such as Soave and Bianco di Custoza.

Lamb

As one of the more affordable meats and one
that is acceptable to many religious communities,
lamb features in many ethnic cuisines such as
Indian, Moroccan, and Middle Eastern – *see* World Food.

Offal

With the exception
of oxtail, which calls
for a full-bodied red like
Zinfandel, many offal
dishes such as calf's liver,
kidneys, and sweetbreads
are quite delicate in
flavour. Partner them with
a lighter red like a mature
red Bordeaux, Burgundy,
or Chianti, or a Pinot Noir.

White wines that go with meat

Australian or Alsace Riesling with Thai beef salad.

Mâcon-Villages Chardonnay with boiled beef.

Sauvignon Blanc with grilled lamb marinated in olive oil, lemon juice, and garlic.

South African Chenin Blanc with cold roast pork.

Reserve California Chardonnay with steak.

...not a white but: pink Champagne with rare roast lamb.

Grilled and roast lamb

safe bets: mature, oaky reds such as red Bordeaux, Chianti, and Spanish reds such as Rioja and Ribera del Duero; Merlot and inexpensive Cabernet Sauvignon.
adventurous alternatives: Greek reds, traditional southern Italian reds such as Copertino and Salice Salentino, and the famous Lebanese red, Chateau Musar.

Lamb shanks and other braised lamb dishes

If cooked in wine drink the same or a similar wine with the dish. Otherwise, go for a characterful medium- to full-bodied French red such as a Côtes du Roussillon, Crozes-Hermitage, or an Argentinian Malbec.

Pork

Like chicken, pork can be equally well accompanied by white wine as red, particularly if it's cooked with a creamy sauce or with fruit such as apples or apricots. Fruity reds work better with sweet or smoky barbecue sauces.
safe bets: dry whites pair well with pork roasted Italian style in white wine (try Italian whites); roast pork with apple sauce and cold roast pork work well with Chardonnay or Chenin Blanc. If you prefer a red, drink a good Beaujolais, Côtes du Rhône, or fruity Merlot.

Pork with cream and mushrooms

safe bet: lightly oaked Chardonnay.
adventurous alternatives: Viognier; Alsace, New Zealand, or Oregon Pinot Gris.

Stir-fried pork, and sweet and sour dishes
safe bets: fruity whites such as Australian Semillon.
adventurous alternatives: Australian or Argentinian rosé.

Spare ribs
safe bets: rich, full-on reds like Chilean Cabernet or California Zinfandel.

Sausages
safe bets: sausage dishes suit rustic southern French blends of Syrah, Grenache, Cinsaut, and Mourvèdre; Spanish reds too.
adventurous alternative: South African Pinotage.

Ham, gammon, and bacon
safe bets: Chablis, unoaked Chardonnay, Merlot, Beaujolais.
adventurous alternative: Australian Semillon.

Charcuterie

French-style
(saucisson, pâté, rillettes, and terrines)

Beaujolais and other French country reds (Gamay, Merlot) or dry southern French white.

Italian-style (salami, prosciutto, etc)

Dry Italian whites; Valpolicella, Dolcetto, authentic red Lambrusco.

Spanish-style (serrano ham, chorizo, etc)

Fino or manzanilla sherry, Spanish *rosado*, unoaked white Rioja, or other dry Spanish whites.

Where to start with chicken? There are so many different ways of cooking it that you're having to match virtually every flavour in the book. Two wines that will generally cope are Chardonnay and Pinot Noir, but if you want to be a bit more adventurous try some of the suggestions below:

chicken & other birds

Organic and free-range chicken

Unlike most mass-produced chicken, organic chicken really does have some flavour, so don't disguise it with too powerful or full-bodied a wine. You might also want to drink a wine that's organic – the Rhône and southern France are areas that offer plenty to choose from.

Plainly roast or grilled chicken
safe bets: red or white Burgundy, or other Chardonnays or Pinot Noirs.
adventurous alternatives: Chianti or other top-quality, fruity Italian reds.

Chicken kiev and other fried chicken
safe bets: sharp citrussy whites like Sauvignon Blanc; unoaked Chardonnays; light reds such as Merlot, Gamay, and Valpolicella.

Chargrilled chicken with herbs, or salads
safe bets: Provençal or Languedoc rosé has the right feel.
adventurous alternatives: Spanish *rosado* from Navarra; Semillon or Semillon/Chardonnay.

Mediterranean-style tomato-based sauces or sauces with onions and peppers
safe bets: Languedoc reds such as Corbières, Minervois,

and Faugères; Rhône reds, Syrah, or Shiraz.
adventurous alternatives: modern Sicilian or Puglian reds.

Lime, coriander, and other Asian flavours
safe bets: New Zealand or Australian Sauvignon Blanc,
Australian Riesling or Verdelho.
adventurous alternatives: Alsace or Chilean Gewurztraminer.

Creamy, white-wine-based, or cheese sauces
safe bets: unoaked or lightly oaked Chardonnay, Alsace
Pinot Blanc, New Zealand, or Oregon Pinot Gris.
adventurous alternatives: Viognier, Roussanne.

Chicken cooked in red wine, like coq au vin
safe bets: red Burgundy is traditional but Rhône reds
work well too.
adventurous alternatives: New World wines from the red
Burgundy grape – California or New Zealand Pinot Noir.

Sweet and sour or fruity dishes
safe bets: fruity whites such as Semillon,
Semillon/Chardonnay, and Australian Riesling;
light, fruity reds such as Merlot.
adventurous alternative: Australian Tarrango.

Smoky barbecue sauces
safe bets: Zinfandel, Argentinian Malbec, South African
Pinotage, Australian Shiraz and Shiraz blends.

Foie gras

Sauternes is the traditional wine to serve with foie gras but not everyone enjoys drinking a sweet wine with a savoury dish. Alternatives to try are Alsace Pinot Gris or Gewurztraminer, a dry Muscat, or a full-bodied Pinot Noir.

You can also drink sweet wines with a smooth duck or chicken liver pâté.

Chinese-style sweet and sour chicken dishes and mild curries

safe bet: Australian Semillon/Chardonnay.
adventurous alternatives: New World Cabernet or Syrah-based rosés, or Bordeaux or Bergerac rosé.

Turkey

...calls for very similar wines to chicken, but because it's usually served on a festive occasion you may want to trade up and bring in something a little more special:
Christmas and Thanksgiving whites: good white Burgundy, or try an Australian, California, New Zealand, or South African Chardonnay.
adventurous alternative: Champagne!
Christmas and Thanksgiving reds: St-Emilion, Pomerol, and other good Merlots; Zinfandel, Australian Shiraz.
adventurous alternative: an Australian sparkling red – Shiraz or Cabernet Sauvignon.

Duck

safe bets: Pinot Noir is the wine that generally goes best with duck – light red Burgundies such as Chorey-lès-Beaune, Marsannay, and Rully with simply cooked roast or pan-fried duck, or more robust Pinots from New Zealand, Oregon, and California if there is a fruity sauce involved.

adventurous alternatives: off-dry German Spätlese Riesling or Australian Semillon can work well if the duck is cooked with orange. More robust rustic reds such as Cahors, Madiran, and Côtes de Roussillon would suit duck confit or duck with olives.

Goose
...needs a wine with a touch of sharpness:
safe bets: Italian reds such as Barolo or Barbaresco, good red Burgundy, or other Pinot Noirs.
adventurous alternatives: German Spätlese Riesling; Alsace Grand Cru Riesling and Gewurztraminer.

Guineafowl
Similar, though slightly gamier than chicken. Follow recommendations below for pheasant.

Pheasant, pigeon (squab), other game birds
Simply roast pheasant is one of the best foils for good-quality, mature red wines.
safe bets: mature red Bordeaux, Barolo, Barbaresco, red Burgundy, Chianti Riserva, Rioja Reserva, aged Cabernet, Syrah or Shiraz.
adventurous alternatives: if served with an intense wine sauce, try a more full-bodied red such as a good Chilean or California Merlot, or Western Australian Cabernet. If it's cooked with apples, go for a German or Alsace Riesling.

Eight extravagant wines for game

Côte-Rôtie

Chambolle-Musigny

Rioja Gran Reserva

Bandol

Barbaresco

Barolo

Bordeaux Crus Classés

Top Tuscan wines such as Sassicaia and Tignanello

Even if you're not a card-carrying veggie there are so many tempting vegetable-based dishes these days that you're bound to end up choosing wine to go with them. (*See* also the Soups, Salads, Eggs, and the World Food section.)

vegetables & veggie dishes

Big bold veg!

If you serve a strongly flavoured vegetable such as braised red cabbage with a meat dish you'll need a more full-bodied wine than if the accompanying vegetables are quite plain: for reds, Syrah or Shiraz, say, rather than Pinot Noir.

It's the cooking that counts

Vegetables have just the same relationship to wine as any other ingredient: they can affect your wine choice, it just depends how you cook them. Raw and lightly cooked (steamed, microwaved, or lightly boiled) vegetables generally call for light-bodied white wines. Vegetables cooked with a creamy- or cheese-based sauce tend to work well with Chardonnay and other smooth dry whites.

More robustly flavoured vegetables like aubergines, peppers, mushrooms, and vegetables that are chargrilled or roasted, generally work better with red wines.

Artichokes

safe bets: none. Artichokes are a notorious wine killer.
avoid: red wine.
adventurous alternatives: Italian whites such as Orvieto or Verdicchio dei Castelli de Jesi will just about see you through, particularly if the artichokes are dressed with a vinaigrette seasoned with a little lemon zest.

Asparagus

safe bets: Sauvignon if the asparagus is served with a
(not too acid) vinaigrette; unoaked Chardonnay if it's served
with a hollandaise sauce or melted butter.
adventurous alternatives: dry Muscat or Alsace Riesling.
Light reds such as Beaujolais can work if you chargrill
the asparagus and serve it with Parmesan shavings.

Aubergines

safe bets: rustic reds such as Fitou, Côtes du Roussillon,
Sicilian reds, and Tempranillo.
adventurous alternatives: Moroccan or (especially for
moussaka) Greek reds. Zinfandel. Crisp dry whites and rosés
with cold aubergine dishes such as baba ganoush.

Cabbage

...can develop a slightly pickled, vinegary flavour with long
cooking which is counteracted by wines with a touch of
sweetness. With sauerkraut (*choucroute*) try a dry Alsace
or German Riesling; with red cabbage a fruity red such
as Dolcetto, Kékfrankos, or Merlot.

Fennel

safe bets: Dry Italian whites like Orvieto; oaked Sauvignon.

Mushrooms

Raw or marinated in salads...
safe bets: unoaked Chardonnay or dry Italian whites such
as Soave or Lugana.

Beans and lentils

Dishes that include beans or lentils are generally quite rustic and work best with hearty reds such as Syrah, Grenache, Corbières, Côtes du Roussillon, Fitou, Minervois, St-Chinian, and wines from the southern Rhône. Also inexpensive Spanish and Portuguese reds, and Spanish and French rosés. Black beans or treacly Boston Baked beans need a sweeter red like Australian Shiraz, Ruby Cabernet, or Zinfandel.

Cooked in cream or in a quiche

safe bets: whites as above or a good Pinot Noir.

luxury option: with wild mushrooms serve a top red Burgundy such as Vosne-Romanée or Chambolle-Musigny, or a California or New Zealand Pinot Noir.

Stuffed with garlic and parsley

safe bets: full-bodied reds such as Zinfandel, Chilean or other New World Cabernet, Merlot, or Shiraz.

Onions

Raw onions are tough on any wine. If they're in a salad, crisp dry whites work best – or New World rosé.

Stuffed, roasted, or caramelised as in a confit or savoury tart tatin

safe bets: soft reds such as Grenache, Tempranillo, and Côtes du Rhône.

Peppers

A component of many Mediterranean-style dishes so they tend to go with Mediterranean wines, particularly dry Italian and southern French whites and rosés, and (especially with cooked pepper dishes like ratatouille) medium-bodied reds.

safe bets: Côtes du Roussillon, Côtes du Rhône, Gigondas, southern French Syrah, Tempranillo, Merlot, Spanish (rosé).

adventurous alternatives: Spanish Albariño, Australian Verdelho, California or southern French Viognier (especially with red pepper soup).

Pumpkin and butternut squash

Quite sweet-flavoured even when being used in a savoury
dish so needs a wine with some character.
safe bets: California Chardonnay or Viognier; Shiraz.
adventurous alternatives: Dolcetto, good Valpolicella.

Spinach and other leafy greens

...have a strong irony taste that goes better with dry
whites than reds, particularly if combined with eggs or
cheese as in a quiche.
safe bets: unoaked Chardonnay, dry Italian whites such
as Soave and Gavi, inexpensive Sicilian whites.
adventurous alternative: with a *spanakopitta* (spinach
and feta cheese pie) try a Greek dry white.

Sweetcorn

safe bets: oaked Chardonnay. There is a real affinity there!

Tomatoes

Raw or lightly cooked
safe bets: Pinot Grigio, Frascati, and other dry Italian
whites; southern French or Spanish rosés; Sauvignon Blanc
(particularly with raw tomato salsas).
Robustly cooked, with herbs and garlic, or with cheese
safe bets: inexpensive southern French and Spanish reds;
Montepulciano d'Abruzzo and other inexpensive Italian
reds; unoaked Syrah.
adventurous alternatives: New World Sangiovese, Sicilian
and Sardinian reds.

It might sound far-fetched to choose a wine to match to a herb or spice but some have a real affinity with a particular grape variety or style of wine.

spices, herbs, & seasonings

Potential winekillers

Problems for wine are created by ingredients that are unusually sweet, sour, hot, or salty:

Habanero and Thai bird's eye chillies.

Vinegar, especially sharp vinaigrettes.

Horseradish, wasabi, and English mustard.

Pickles and chutneys.

Raw garlic (or onion).

Salted anchovies.

Basil (particularly pesto)
safe bets: dry Italian whites such as Soave, Bianco di Custoza, Gavi, and Lugana; light unoaked Chardonnays.

Coriander (fresh) and dill
safe bet: Sauvignon Blanc.

Mediterranean herbs: thyme, rosemary, oregano
safe bets: rustic reds like Côtes de Roussillon and Corbières.
adventurous alternatives: Greek reds.

Mint
safe bet: Try Cabernet Sauvignon, it has a real affinity with mint.
adventurous alternatives: dry whites such as Sauvignon Blanc are better with Middle Eastern-style dishes.

Tarragon
safe bet: unoaked Chardonnay.
adventurous alternatives: French blends of Roussanne, Marsanne, and Viognier; Arneis (from northern Italy).

Chillies

Very hot chillies cause problems for wine but crisp, fruity whites such as Sauvignon are OK. The dried chillies in Mexican or southwest American food are better with more full-bodied Chilean or California reds.

Garlic (as in chicken kiev, or garlic butter)

safe bets: Sauvignon or inexpensive unoaked Chardonnays.
adventurous alternatives: Italian reds, Teroldego Rotaliano.

Ginger (especially in oriental dishes)

safe bets: aromatic whites such as Alsace or Chilean Gewurztraminer, Riesling, and, curiously, Champagne.

Mustard (as in rabbit with mustard sauce)

safe bets: Dijon mustard is the most wine-friendly type and goes well with lighter Burgundies – white and red.
adventurous alternatives: unoaked Chardonnays, Rioja.

Paprika/pimenton (as in goulash)

safe bets: Eastern and central European reds, eg Kékfrankos.
adventurous alternatives: Tempranillo, southern French reds.

Pepper (as in steak au poivre)

safe bets: juicy, full-bodied young New World reds.
avoid: very oaky wines made of Syrah or Shiraz.

Salt (as in anchovies, salt cod, salt beef)

Tricky – but very dry, unoaked, whites just about work.

Luxury items

Truffles are highly scented and have an overwhelming influence. Black truffles go with the sort of wines that work with game – red Burgundy and aged Barolo. White truffles are good with vivid, young Italian reds like Dolcetto.

Saffron (as in paella, risotto Milanese, etc) goes with dry whites such as Soave, Gavi, or Albariño. Or Spanish *rosado*, or young Tempranillo.

The cardinal rule is that your wine should be sweeter than your dessert – which makes fruity desserts the easiest to match, and cold ones easier than hot ones. Also, chill the wine to counteract the sweetness – an hour and a half in the fridge at least.

fruity puddings

Fruit in wine

Rather than drinking wine with your fruit you can always pour it over the top – or poach the fruit in it. Combinations that work are pears or plums in red wine, ripe peaches in Champagne, and strawberries served with a light red such as Beaujolais.

Sweet wines that taste best on their own

Very expensive, super-sweet wines like German or Austrian Trockenbeerenausleses and Eiswein, or Canadian Icewine, are better chilled and sipped on their own. Or served with a few cantucci biscuits.

Apples and pears

Simple tarts are the ideal desserts to pair with sweet wine.
safe bets: sweet Loire wines such as Coteaux du Layon, *moelleux* Vouvray, Bonnezeaux, Quarts de Chaume; sweet Bordeaux, late harvest Semillon.

Peaches and nectarines

Can be poached in wine, have wine poured over them (*see* left) but are also sublime with...
safe bets: Sauternes and cheaper options such as Monbazillac and Saussignac, and with Muscat de Beaumes-de-Venise.
adventurous alternative: demi-sec Champagne.

Strawberries

safe bets: Moscato d'Asti (if served on their own); Premières Côtes de Bordeaux and other inexpensive sweet Bordeaux, or late harvest Semillon (if with cream).

Apricots

safe bets: Muscat, late harvest Riesling. Tokáji if served hot.

Raspberries

safe bet: late harvest Rieslings (better still if you add cream).
adventurous alternative: raspberry liqueur topped up with
Champagne or sparkling wine, with raspberry sauce or coulis.

Blackberries, blackcurrants, and blueberries

Sharpness makes them tricky. Late harvest Rieslings go best.

Gooseberries

safe bet: very good with Muscat de Beaumes-de-Venise.

Lemon-flavoured desserts

safe bet: very sharply flavoured lemon tarts are hard to
match, but sweet Rieslings should cope.

Orange-flavoured desserts

safe bets: inexpensive French, Spanish, or Greek Muscat.

Pineapple and other tropical fruits

safe bets: late harvest or botrytis Riesling or Semillon.

Fruit salads

safe bets: Moscato d'Asti or Asti.
adventurous alternatives: sweet Riesling or Gewurztraminer.

Dried fruits, such as raisins, figs, and dates

safe bets: fortified wines like tawny port, sweet oloroso
sherries, and sweet Madeiras. These wines work well with
fruit cakes such as Christmas cake too.

Budget sweet wines

Moscatel de Valencia

Southern French Muscats
such as Muscat de
Rivesaltes and Muscat
de Frontigan

Greek Samos Muscat

Mavrodaphne of Patras
(a Greek sweet red –
good with chocolate)

Moscato d'Asti

Australian late harvest
Riesling or Semillon

Luxury sweet wines

Sauternes and Barsac

Vin Santo

German or Austrian
Trockenbeerenauslese

Bonnezeaux or Quarts de
Chaume from the Loire

Eiswein or Icewine

Be in the know

Adding cream to a sharply
flavoured fruit makes
it more wine-friendly.
So does serving it with
meringues.

Drinking a sweet wine with something as sweet as chocolate might seem like too much of a good thing but the experience can be so sublime you should occasionally indulge.

other sweet things

Desserts that flatter sweet wines

Simple French-style fruit or frangipane tarts

Fresh peaches or nectarines

Crème brûlée or pannacotta

Sweet wines that flatter desserts

Don't overlook sweet sparkling wines such as Moscato d'Asti, demi-sec Champagne, and fortified wines such as sweet sherries and port. You might think they'd be too strong to partner a dessert but you only need a small glass.

Creamy desserts (crème brûlée, pannacotta, light cheesecakes...)

safe bets: Sweet Bordeaux, especially Sauternes, late harvest Semillon, most Muscats (but if they accompany fruit, match the wine to the fruit.)

Light airy desserts (soufflés, creamy gateaux, and roulades)

safe bet: sweet (demi-sec or *doux*) Champagne.
adventurous alternative: sparkling Vouvray.

Caramel, toffee, and nut flavoured desserts

safe bets: if light, like crème caramel or an almond tart, an inexpensive Muscat should work. With richer flavoured desserts like pecan pie or sticky toffee pudding try an Australian liqueur Muscat.
adventurous alternative: 10-year old tawny port.

Honey flavoured desserts

safe bets: inexpensive Muscats – so long as the dessert is not too sweet. Otherwise Australian liqueur Muscat.

Chocolate

safe bets: none... especially with dark, rich, molten chocolate desserts.

adventurous alternatives: sweet red wines such as Black Muscat, Mavrodaphne of Patras, and Recioto (a sweet Valpolicella); Banyuls and Maury (French *vin doux naturels*) work reasonably well too. As do liqueur Muscats if you have a very sweet tooth. And Orange Muscat can be good with white chocolate or milk chocolate desserts.

Hot puddings (bread and butter pudding, Christmas pudding)

safe bets: inexpensive dessert wines such as Greek or southern French Muscat.

adventurous alternatives: Hungarian Tokaji, Passito di Pantelleria.

Ice-creams & sorbets

Served on their own these can be tricky to match. Only really rich viscous wines like liqueur Muscat (great with toffee crunch ice-cream) or sweet oloroso or PX sherry (try with vanilla) really work. But if it accompanies a pud, not a problem.

If you've ever wondered why your favourite wine doesn't go with the cheese you're eating, the answer is that cheese and wine isn't the miracle match it's made out to be. So if you're a cheese lover and have piled the board with a huge selection of different cheeses, watch out!

cheese to please

Budget all-rounder cheese matchers

Copertino (southern Italy)

Valdepeñas (Spain)

Chilean Cabernet/Merlot

Romanian Pinot Noir

Aged Bulgarian Cabernet Sauvignon

Creating a cheeseboard

The hardest cheeses to match are, regrettably, some of the most interesting ones. Very ripe, runny cheeses, well-matured hard cheeses like Cheddar, and blue cheeses such as Gorgonzola and Roquefort are all tricky customers. If these are among your favourites it's much better to serve them individually, with a wine that will stand up to the battering, rather than to ruin a good bottle.

By contrast it's much easier to match mild cheeses, particularly waxy ones such as Gouda, Jarlsberg, and Comté, or to serve a fine wine with a good piece of Parmesan.

You can also make your cheeseboard more wine-friendly by serving walnut bread and a selection of dried fruits with it.

Having said that, there are some good all-rounders that will cope with a number of different cheeses: Italian Amarone, Rioja Reserva and other aged Spanish reds, red wines from the Douro in Portugal, Grenache and Grenache-dominated wines such as those from the southern Rhône and Languedoc, mature Syrah and Shiraz, tawny and vintage port, aged amontillado sherry, ten-year old and Bual Madeira.

White or bloomy rind cheeses such as Camembert and Brie

safe bets (so long as the cheese isn't too ripe): soft, fruity reds such as Chilean or other New World Merlot, California or New Zealand Pinot Noir, good Valpolicella.
adventurous alternatives: Dolcetto or Loire reds such as Bourgueil and Saumur-Champigny.

Hard cheeses such as Cheddar, Lancashire, and traditional English cheeses

safe bets: medium- to full-bodied reds without too much tannin such as Rioja, St-Emilion and softer styles of Bordeaux, good quality Côtes du Rhône-Villages, Shiraz/Syrah, and Grenache. Oaked Chardonnay can also be surprisingly good.

Blue cheeses

Inclined to be troublesome partners for any wine apart from the classic partnerships of Roquefort and Sauternes, and port and Stilton.
adventurous alternatives: Hungarian Tokaji, Australian liqueur Muscat, ten-year old Madeira, Mavrodaphne of Patras.

Before or after dessert?

Whether you have your cheese French-style before dessert, or after, is a matter of choice, but one that can also depend on the wine and the cheese you're serving. If you're drinking a good red it makes sense to follow the main course immediately with cheese, but if you're serving cheeses like Roquefort that go better with a sweet or fortified wine, you may prefer to leave them till the end of the meal.

Strong, smelly cheeses

safe bets: none. Better kept away from your best bottles, particularly fragile old Bordeaux and Burgundy.
adventurous alternatives: again, sweet or fortified wines are likely to do best of all. Or aromatic whites, as in the traditional pairing of Munster and Gewurztraminer. If you still want to serve a red, try one with a touch of porty sweetness like an Amarone, a Douro red, or a late harvest Zinfandel.

Very rich creamy cheeses such as Vacherin

Not easy. Try California or New Zealand Pinot Noir.

Goat's cheeses

safe bet: Sauvignon Blanc is a really good match with most goat's cheeses, especially young, soft ones.
adventurous alternatives: English dry whites, Rueda (from Spain).

Sheep's cheeses

safe bets: robust southern French reds such as Corbières, Costières de Nîmes, and Pic St-Loup, Madiran, and wines made from the Syrah, Mourvèdre, Grenache, and Tempranillo grapes.
adventurous alternatives: Corsican or Sardinian reds. Or if you want to experiment with a sweet wine, a southern French Muscat or late harvest Riesling.

Smoked cheeses

safe bets: no totally safe bet!
adventurous alternatives: Morio Muskat, and other
inexpensive Muscats.

Hot cheese dishes

Cheese immediately adds a richness to a dish that
can make full-bodied, jammy reds such as Australian
Shiraz, California or Chilean Cabernet Sauvignon, seem
cloying. In general it's better to serve a wine with a
touch of sharpness that will cut through any sensation
of oiliness or fattiness.
safe bets: Italian reds such as Barbera and Chianti work
particularly well with meat dishes such as lasagne,
cannelloni and moussaka (as do other Sangioveses and
inexpensive young Syrahs and Merlots.)
adventurous alternatives: Zinfandel, Primitivo, or a
Greek red.

White wines can work with lighter dishes such as quiches,
pasta bakes, or pancakes with cheese, and cheese fondue
(a classic partnership with crisp dry Swiss whites like
Chasselas or whites from the Savoie region.)
safe bets: unoaked and lightly oaked Chardonnays from
cooler regions such as northern Italy, Burgundy, southern
France (Limoux), and Chile. Also Alsace Pinot Blanc and
Italian Soave.

White wines that go with cheese

Sancerre and goat's cheese

Oaked Chardonnay and
Cheddar

Chasselas and cheese
fondue

Chablis and Chaource

Sauvignon Blanc with
garlic and herb roulé

It isn't often that a wine dictates a meal but there are occasions when a celebration may take the form of a special bottle. The most obvious are romantic occasions – such as Valentine's Day or an anniversary – when Champagne is likely to be the order of the day.

special wines

Personalize your choice

A wine may be special but it won't be a treat unless the person you're celebrating with is going to enjoy it. Not everyone likes Champagne, for example (crazy mad fools!). If you don't already know the tastes of the person you're trying to impress, try and do a bit of detective work beforehand.

Making the stars shine

The main thing is not to overdo it and serve rich, fussy food alongside great wine. The cardinal rule is Keep it Simple.

If a bottle has been kept for any length of time it's likely to be in quite a fragile state so don't overwhelm it with strong spices and seasonings, or over-rich sauces. In fact, with older bottles it's always as well to have a fall-back in reserve that will also go with the meal you're cooking just in case the wine turns out to be corked, or simply past it.

And don't serve too powerful a wine first so that your star bottle seems faded by comparison – for example, oaky rich Chardonnay before an old claret. It's better to drink a classy but neutral wine so that you build up to your special bottle.

Champagne

Most people treat **Champagne** as a pre-dinner drink but if it's a good enough bottle it can easily take you right through

ON-CHARLEM

GRAND CRU

APPELLATION CONTRÔLÉE

du Mart

a meal. Fizz-friendly foods include most kinds of seafood, especially shellfish, and luxury fish such as turbot and halibut, as well as caviar and smoked salmon (the finer cut the salmon and the more delicate the smoke, the better.)

Aged vintage Champagne also has a honeyed richness that works well with truffles and mushrooms, and even with game such as pigeon and wild duck if it's cooked relatively rare and not too heavily sauced. You can also drink **vintage rosé Champagne** with rare roast beef and lamb.

A glass of **sweet** (demi-sec or *doux*) **Champagne** is a glamourous way to finish off a meal, especially with a birthday – or other celebratory – cake.

Great whites

Chances are that if you've spent a fair bit on a bottle of white, it's going to be **Chardonnay** – either a New World one or a **top white Burgundy**. Again, think in terms of luxury shellfish such as lobster, langoustines, or crab, or even oysters – if you add a squeeze of lemon. Creamy sauces – either on fish, or on chicken, or guineafowl – also flatter Chardonnay.

The other great white grape, is **Riesling**. It's not the easiest variety to match but it is a good partner for smoked fish and meat, and for Asian-inspired dishes, particularly if it has a touch of sweetness. (Look out for **German Spätlese** and aged Rieslings from **Alsace**.)

a meal. Fizz-friendly foods include most kinds of seafood, especially shellfish, and luxury fish such as turbot and halibut, as well as caviar and smoked salmon (the finer cut the salmon and the more delicate the smoke, the better.)

Aged vintage Champagne also has a honeyed richness that works well with truffles and mushrooms, and even with game such as pigeon and wild duck if it's cooked relatively rare and not too heavily sauced. You can also drink **vintage rosé Champagne** with rare roast beef and lamb.

A glass of **sweet** (demi-sec or *doux*) **Champagne** is a glamourous way to finish off a meal, especially with a birthday – or other celebratory – cake.

Great whites

Chances are that if you've spent a fair bit on a bottle of white, it's going to be **Chardonnay** – either a New World one or a **top white Burgundy**. Again, think in terms of luxury shellfish such as lobster, langoustines, or crab, or even oysters – if you add a squeeze of lemon. Creamy sauces – either on fish, or on chicken, or guineafowl – also flatter Chardonnay.

The other great white grape, is **Riesling**. It's not the easiest variety to match but it is a good partner for smoked fish and meat, and for Asian-inspired dishes, particularly if it has a touch of sweetness. (Look out for **German Spätlese** and aged Rieslings from **Alsace**.)

Great reds

The fantastic thing about serving a brilliant bottle of red is that it lets you completely off the hook. All you have to do is serve a simple steak, grill, or roast and everyone's happy.

That said, there are a couple of points to remember. Expensive young reds will have a lot of concentration and tannin to accommodate, so you can be quite robust in your cooking method – roasting, searing, chargrilling, or even barbecuing. Older vintages are more delicate and match subtler flavours better – simply roast lamb, for instance, or feathered game.

The grape also makes a difference. Good **Pinot Noir** (red **Burgundy** especially) is generally lighter-bodied than top **Cabernet** or **Syrah**, so is a better choice for lighter meats such as chicken, guineafowl, pheasant, grouse, or partridge.

Sublime sweet wines

Some wines – such as **Vin Santo**, or **Austrian** or **German Trockenbeerenausleses** – are so intense they're better sipped on their own or with some ripe, luscious fruit like a peach. But for the most part, the world's top sweet wines taste best with a simple fruit tart (especially apple and pear tarts), or a creamy pudding like a crème brûlée.

Sauternes is also traditionally paired with Roquefort or with foie gras but such dramatic sweet-savoury combinations are not to everyone's taste. If you want to make a special fuss of a wine lover though, this is the way to their heart!

Decanting

You don't need to decant most young red wines – only those which are old and unfiltered and likely to have thrown a deposit – but it does look impressive. Oak-aged whites, strangely enough, can also benefit. Leave the bottle upright for twenty-four hours then place a light behind it and pour carefully and steadily into the decanter until any sediment reaches the neck. Then stop immediately but don't stop midway!

index